# .negrophobia.

White Man's World. Black Man's Culture.
Prose. Plots. Politics. Poems.

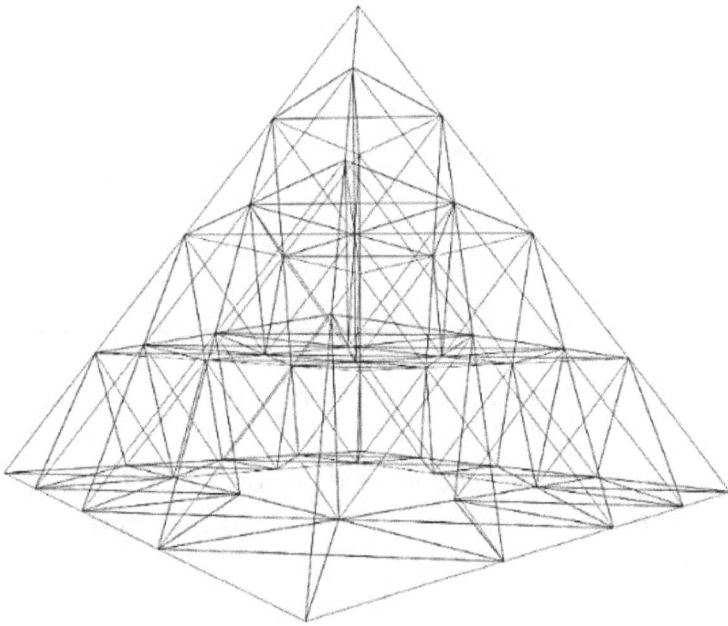

## Andre R. Fields, Ph.D.

IAAP Publishing
The Institute of African American Psychology

# IAAP Publishing

FOR INFORMATION:

IAAP Publishing
PHONE: 616.323.8506
EMAIL: afields@theiaap.org
WEBSITE: www.theiaap.org

.negrophobia.
Prose. Plots. Politics. Poems.

Copyright © 2020 by Andre R. Fields, Ph.D.

Printed in the United States of America
A catalog record of this book is available from the Library of Congress.

ISBN: 978-0-578-69956-1 (IAAP)

# THE INSTITUTE
# OF
# AFRICAN AMERICAN
# PSYCHOLOGY

## (IAAP)

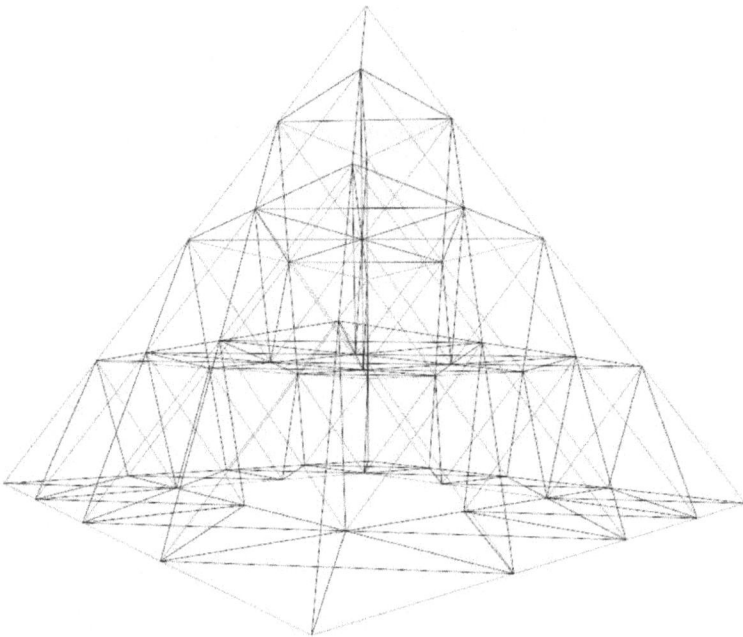

www.theiaap.org

*To the pawns, protestors, and political prisoners.*

*Read each line slowly and with intentionality...*

**Negro (n).**

1. A member of a dark-skinned group of peoples originally native to the continent of Africa.

**Phobia (n).**

1. An extreme or irrational fear of or aversion to something.

**Negrophobia (n).**

1. To possess an extreme conscious and subconscious fear of Black Americans.
2. To harbor an unwarranted dread and concern about the potential experiencing of a loss of power as a result of Black American progress.
3. The repeated experiencing of paralyzing anxiety at the thought of suffering a loss of resources as a result of Black American progress.
4. The irrational unwillingness to engage in power sharing with Black Americans.
5. The tendency to engage in discriminatory practices for the sake of blocking the social progress of Black Americans.

# .negrophobia.

# The End Is Over

I fantasize a romantic death

Make love to the ugly world with my last breaths

Homicide in the Crystal Cathedral they shattered me

My motion picture is a comedy…a tragedy

The symphony in the synagogue in slow motion

Fast forward the movie of life we are so hopeless

How can we ever beat the game the game is hard

How can we ever cheat the game the game is God

Holy wars and sacred crusades with invisible ghost

Lurk in the halls of the Vatican with the ghost of the pope

Spit venom voodoo priest with holy whispers

Throw hexes with street religion and broken scriptures

I can draw you a vision dark pictures

Tattoos on Black dudes hieroglyphics

# The Day Before The Morning After

Daddy spoke somewhat distinguished with broken English

Ghetto slang in intervals as he held his penis

Was born in Eden died in Babylon awoke on Venus

Shot dope intravenous pops was leaking with hopeless semen

In mommy he skeeted drunken style dramatic form

A haunted night of climatic storms a star was born

Traumatic dawns beyond the scorn between an eclipse

The day before the morning after I swore to be rich

The blessed sperm stepped in a germ these lessons I learn

Last night Satan came to me told me I was destined to burn

On crossroads with lost souls on infinity's trip

With bullet holes who'd ever thought they would empty the clip

Pronounced dead in a code of silence a quiet end

Came all this way from the other side to die again

The FDA injects diabetes in our urban system of water

I drank from the faucet so yes I'll be counted in the slaughter

Dr. Kevorkian's Klansmen in white medical jackets bleed IVs into our fathers

Built PTSD into our minds and injected HIV into our daughters

Prisoners to patriotism our jail bars are stars and stripes

Married to the game estranged wedlock a bastard's plight

We tried to escape but they trafficked our beings and carried us to this grave

Chained our spirits to a rock and left our souls in America's cave

They abused our physicality and subjected our desires to shame

Forced to embrace a demonic pain using our bodies as spare parts for the game

A Black man's tragic eulogy is a White man's sinister conspiracy

George Floyd's memory is screaming for momma somewhere in eternity

The government is just 1 puppet on the strings of the devil's leash

Expendable…pawns of society our role as a chess piece

A political illuminati has purposely poisoned this utopia

White tribalism, incensed by hate, they cheat us for hopes of racial euphoria

Please don't ask God to send the world a sign I'll send you our tears

Tell the political illuminati to please beware…the revolution is here

# Negrophobia

Be very-very still you are under surveillance

By KGB, the FBI, and Central Intelligence

How we became slaves to the game is now irrelevant

Today they give us pain and some fame for medicine

We are now forever addicted to this

Sell our souls for a hit...harlot our bodies for chips

This is the last blow I will hit

A perpetual relapse ignorance is bliss

American nightmare a dream world of false societies

It's oh so real...real talk reality

We were not meant for this...we were tricked into this shit

White society is sick...blasphemously ridiculous

The fearful are aware of us indeed they are scared of us

This is exactly why they don't care for us

They yearn for our clan to suicide

But before that we will maniacally homicide

This is 100 percent straight talk I do not have to lie

And I will not have an alibi

Illustrated souls on the pages of a comic book that God drew

Turn the pages as Morgan Freeman narrates the life of our cartoon

It's an oppressive adventure insanely bizarre...oh so loony tune

The riddles of discrimination so many clues...I'm so confused

No solace or tranquility but still we believe in the mystery

Sworn to secrecy a treacherous allegiance it's all a conspiracy

Negroes wear chains like nooses with charms shaped like the Pentagon

How stupid can you be...they are the ones trying to get rid of y'all

We scurry for crumbs in the ghetto like rats in a sweltering maze

They ignite our fears and trigger our rage then leave guns in our cage

Drunk off emotion we pick up artillery stumbling in a daze

Hate ourselves...kill our own brothers...drive-bys in an intoxicating haze

Government corruption Reaganomics put drugs in the ghetto

Not to mention crack, heroin, gangsta rap, mental illness, and of course the devil

From X, MLK, to JFK they killed all of our glorious rebels

The time has come, impregnate our queens...we must breed more rebels

Stone warlord on a bronze horse frozen in time's freezer

Statue of a war...a battle icon holding a 9 millimeter

For space invaders that hate a player trail me in cabs

In black trenches and white glove with alien masks

Running desperate through the centuries from sociopaths

The sons of my enemies obsessively follow my path

Pull guns on my entity threaten to blast

Kingdom will come before they finish me the chosen will last

Peeped ahead in the book of life the scroll cheater

How you think I made it this far the overachiever

The soul believer, Jehovah, Jesus, the called and the chose

Slurred speech with a gangsta lean...Wild Irish Rose

Come from a place far-far away the Arabian visitor

In iron cuffs I followed the stars the Octavian prisoner

The circle of life tree-to-tree I swing in the bubble

Pose on the block like stone lion heads king of the jungle

Electronic android robotics...mechanical shell

Preprogrammed my body goes numb when injured from shells

Metabolic animalistic ferocious tremors

Seductive groans erotic moans soft whispers

Enough pain enough games enough is enough

I want out if life is a bitch I'm stuck in this slut

A grown man walking hungry the starving artist

Looking puzzled in the courtroom this place is haunted

My father figures were Pac and Biggie…now I'm an orphan in tears

Can't stop thuggin so I guess I'm stuck in my childhood years

Romantic, look deep inside the beautiful one

Outlawed the streets don't want me I keep on the run

From BC to AD been stuck in this book

We all know we be crazy and a little bit shook

Stuck in this same hood, with this same moon, and these same stars

Same killers, same tattoos, same scars, and these same cars

Drop the charges in Babylon do us equal

We needed shoes the rent was due…screw you people

Judge's sentence was unhuman…supernatural numbers

Banished to insane asylums they want us under

We are children living in a never-ever ending story

There are no winning, happy ending, magic rainbows, coming for me

Thus, we are sleeping with dreamy eyes believing fairytales and lies

Lullabies and rockabyes sleep tight tonight in the land before time

# Triflin' Death

Young killers soaking in rain outside his crib virtuous patience

Navy seals in army fatigues camouflaged with dirt on their faces

Followed him home then cut off the lights from the phone pole

They nymphos, they sickos, they psychos

Throw pipe bombs through the side door and the front window

Death's debris litters the block it all explodes

House of flames…he stops, drops, and crawls through the emergency exit

They hunt him down like predicons in the jungle for breakfast

Hear deep breaths and footsteps coming "pow-pow" in the leg and the stomach

Hobbling and limping but there is no escape a dead man running

Fell to his knees, then to his face, now circled by bastards

Children surround him with toy blasters and childlike laughter

In the playground Cabrini-Greens the holy recess

He coughed blood they spat on his face with no regrets

He hold on tight but hells angels broke his life out

His body cells imprisoned by Hennessey and a cocaine bout

Rain carries his blood to the sewer along the curb

The ravens circle the cemetery awaiting his return

The demons poke him with pitchforks rip chunks out of his clothes

Sip on his blood like Cristal drunk off his soul

Dismembered corpse left in the street maimed by the dogs

Vultures carry his carcass to the black hills in the maze of the fog

## Religious Wars

Blood soaks his jewelry his soul is on his ice

Thugs in mourning vendetta slugs explode in the night

They séance in the candlelight trying to raise his spirit

Warlords losing their minds they seen the Hygleerix

Rituals sacrifices black magic

Occultic victuals burning torches on the black Sabbath

Summon the gods incarnate morph into cougars

Pray to the darkness, praise the madness, worship karma sutra

Voodoo dolls in the crystal lair hear the roars

Street battles under the flesh religious wars

## The Federal Agenda

More money more problems you know how it is

No money more problems you know how we live

In Oz the Wonderful Wiz the cartel

Masters of time throw bombshells give my people hell

Stars fell from out the skies like meteors

Feds chopped them up…gave them to hustlers…now they in the door

There is plenty more where that came from just look in the galaxies

Stars twinkle and shimmer a code patterned astrology

Horoscopes morphine frozen veins

Kilos in the Eos solar games

Deliveries UFOs Martian vendettas

Space shuttles with supped-up engines marked with bandannas

Leave gang signs in cornfields abduct hood pharaohs

Make pyramids out of crack houses pull your tarot

Sleeping beauty nightingale the ballet sighs

Avalon spoiler alert everybody dies

## Make Love In Hell

My jewels are in the dusts of hell the jewelry box

My passions burn in the fires of hades the fury lox

She left me...said I dream too much I talk in my sleep

Stopped having sex once I heard the voice...she calls me a freak

For weeks and weeks she watched me pace slowly go crazy

Spirits leaping in and out of me they told me she hates me

She finally left via suicide a bottle of pills

I still see her she comes to me at night in the hills

With broken wings trying to lure me see tears through her veil

Says lets hold hands in front of the flames make love in hell

Definition and angle freelance Polaroid

Delusions of grandeur schizophrenic paranoid

They stalk my essence chasing me down with battle cries

The dawn is eerier see the air glow in an apocalyptic sunrise

Dark and dreary looked out the window I saw nirvana

Stepped back closed the curtains divine drama

This here is the end of all life as we've all known it

Murderous ink scribbled in blood of dead poets

Wide awake in the nightmare of fate's glare

In Death's chair on the porch of torture we all stare

Intoxicated on radiation and waste fumes

There is no love…they see blood…they hate you

Underground civilizations ghetto cults

Bomb shelters in abandoned churches metal vaults

Time surrenders space retreats the portals close

Trap doors fall deep…to places no mortal knows

## They Don't Know

God forbid someone read our minds and stole our message

Stripped us down cell by cell until our souls were naked

Like whoa we stressin...cold and sweatin

Suicide in the hotel shower is what our foes expected

But we hold a sacred blessing and a golden weapon

Divine rules and principles our code of ethics

Been in this saga oh so long old and restless

Came to far to turn back now there is no regretting

Dipped our swords in that infinite hole it glows fluorescent

A burning cross with blue flames on a frozen necklace

We must unite at all costs...wireless communications

We ain't lazy...we are just tired to death...new nation

Hands aching from the plantation it's in our genes

We don't want to work no more we just want to dream

Complex they think we're crazy they are right

They don't know, if they only knew, they are right

I saw your pain when you lost your brains to the sawed-off gauge

Arteries and veins graffitied the bricks I read your lost page

Demon laughter trying to snatch your ether as your head bled

But we prayed and I know you repented on your deathbed

Eyes rolled he died in my arms it's like I'm still there

Hail Mary he disappeared into thin air

In mid-air I drew a cross with my right palm

Head-to-chest…shoulder-to-shoulder for his ride home

Took his charm cracked the concrete with glass tears

Looked in the night sky…blew a kiss to my dawg…and laughed at my fears

Stood to my feet ripped of my shirt fondled my pearls

Shot 17 bullets towards the full moon screamed, "Fuck the world!"

Why my people die so young we just came out the dust

Can still smell the dirt on our skin…Lord who do we trust

One question, "Are our struggles part of your plan or did they catch you slippin?"

"Are you away on another planet on another mission?"

"Forgot us down here on earth…down here turning"

"Down here hurt…down here squirming"

"Precious Lord hear my prayer from a Sinner's perspective"

"I informed the angels but evidently, they didn't give you the message"

"Why do we suffer so long die so early?"

"Racing time on this ancient planet before evolution deserts me."

"Dark tomorrows the future is bleak no luck in this game."

"You're God, everywhere at once, can't move, you're like us, stuck in the game."

"You know the past, future, and present the windows and doors"

"It seems to me, I don't know Lord, it just seems like you're bored"

"Hope you feel from a divine angle subatomic complexities"

"For me to exist it is evident at 1 point you were obsessed with me"

"Love fan…you built me…winded me up…then watched me perform"

"Sin-repent-sin-repent…constantly reborn"

"I'm torn between 2 forces love and hatred"

"Running to you I'm torn apart reaching for Satan"

"Hope you still love me after all these questions I hope I ain't blew it"

"For some reason it just seemed right as if you told me to do it"

The Heart Love's Conspiracy Couldn't Break

On all I love, I still believe though at times it is hard

They say we evolved from trillions and trillions of pieces of shards

That probability is so unlikely never listen to man

Complex design and strategy requires a plan

No strategy can ever be conceived without a brain

Or intellect a supreme God constructed the game

Mentally drained thinking way too deep way too 3-D

I am that light shining out the sewer…Lord I know you see me

Oh you gonna ignore me, go ahead and vanish, I will keep on the run

Go ahead and leave, you'll be back, I know you'll miss me for love

# Momma's Little Boy

If I miss and they shoot me first and I fall dead

Tell my momma rep the blood of Christ wear all red

At my wake let it all be said tell her the truth

Heard I was dead but you had to see it...you needed the proof

Now go ahead...do what you came to do...shoot in my casket

I'll get revenge one way or another in the dust and the ashes

I never trusted you bastards you were raised like me

To the top of the cliff poppaless on the edge like me

In class couldn't draw dad when we drew life's picture

Now we know the meaning of heartless but the plot got thicker

30 seconds I can see the light upon my demise

Tell my people to keep fighting keep their heads to the sky

When I die...tell momma don't cry...I want the world to mourn

Because it is finished the game is over the pearl is gone

No more trying to get home anxieties embalmed

At my funeral, don't touch my mom leave her alone

You fakers...don't spit on her bastard respect her prayers

And don't laugh until they close the casket you player haters

## Counterfeit Freedom

Human trafficked chained, twisted, and tossed

All our prophets, disciples, and thugs have been nailed to a cross

Our forefathers hung our daddies hunting season

Never again…never again…we yearn freedom

Come out the dark it's time to shine justice will lead us

We are young children of the night the future leaders

Fuck the system we see the plot we keep getting poorer

They getting richer we getting sicker in this social slaughter

Abandoned infants at America's palace we were found at the gates

Adopted by White devils and Black demons we are childs of the state

Slave trade as babes we were sold on the black market

Capitalism you a product nigga in case you forgot it

Don't ever forget we were slaves for the rich clones on this earth

Spare parts for the super race separated at birth

Freedom is for sell and by any means we must pay the price

Rebel slaves escaping our chains it's time to fight

## The Triangle Theory

I want America to know that I never cared what y'all thought about us

The only thing we ever did wrong was give you all of us

Foolish people we prayed for you devils with scriptures and carols

My theory, the good will die rich, I see it all in the tarots

The US hated us…when all we ever did was try to lead y'all home

Y'all won't appreciate God's chosen until we're raptured and gone

Betrayed by the jury found guilty we lay in our fury

Our prayer is eerie faith will avenge us…the triangle theory

We have nots and bottom dwellers N-word niggers

Cops treat my people like Black Jews…they're our Adolf Hitler

Stuck in the walls between 2 worlds as the banner flies

Sworn to secrecy we pledge allegiance to America's lies

## Hell's Virgins

We act in a play, God watches, while angels applaud

The men in black of your motion picture are devilish frauds

Avoid lust and eye contact with the faces of death

Hell's virgins you stuck in a high who laced your Moet

Black lights flicker chemicals morph your biology

Don't believe it, it is all a trick, reverse psychology

Hormones making whores moan exotic touch

Hell's virgins Bloody Mary hypnotic lust

Time and space is a lucid blur who Mickeyed your juice

Unlocked Pandora's Box the spirits are loose

Gargoyles, goonies, goons, goblins, and feigns

In the spook of the haunted club follow the screams

Saturday night fever the black Sabbath sing in percussion

Shoot up the club make their ears bleed with the strings of destruction

Read their minds they're plotting on you…a quiet riot

Found dead in a slew of violence a moment of silence

As angels fall and your life dies you must learn your mistakes

Incarnate…do it all again…the virgins await

# Mrs. Satana

Be careful what you wish for on those silent nights

Lust brought sin, sin brought death when she entered my life

My heart whimpers I recall her whispers her dark temper

I start to shiver how did I miss the signs of a hot December

Chocolate skin with the scent of a virgin a Black Madonna

Should have known she rose from hell…her name was Satana

Whispered to me, "I love you more than your momma, I'm down for your battle."

But where was she when I started pacing and talking to shadows

A little rattled I fell off my rocker a screw popped loose

Days later I turned suicidal on top of the roof

The voices told me to cock and shoot in the face of the wind

Sex, drugs, and hip-hop have tricked me again

Happy birthday what you want somebody to hug

Happy birthday what you need somebody to love

Your head is beneath the covers you tossing and turning

Another year has passed you by what are you learning

The ghosts of last birthdays past are haunting your home

I know you tired from thinking too much piecing these codes

You been hanging around this town for way too long

Can't feel the spirit when the choir sings it's time to move on

Love hurts especially when he slapping your face

Making hate beneath the sheets you're trapped in a rape

What you thought you were the first he knocked before

He so loved you that he beat his one begotten whore

Forgotten doors open wide curtains raise

Momma was right in her prophesy of rainy days

Today's a blessing but tomorrow's coming…feels like a curse

Too strong to die feel wrong to cry for what it's worth

Happy Birthday baby girl love is the key

Follow your dreams wherever they lead young dove be free

Through your window I see you dancing all alone on your birthday tonight

But joy cometh in the morning my princess sleep tight

# The Visitation

On my way to visit the homie doing a life sentence 200 years fold

When they told me no parole I fell to the flo

Inside the hexagon superstructure they tricking the nation

Institutionalize my people in the prison system a human factory station

Breathing products merchandise human supplies

While the court is a corporation…embezzling lives

Life goes on so once again we have to be strong

Been doing this since they sent those ships…took us from home

Last hours we the last flowers in the wind

In the fields behind the fence in the pen

We can make it, just the 2 of us, if only we try

Fight for your people we meet in the sequel whether dead or alive

I know you lonely on the inside your feelings ain't right

We will escape to the other side through the tunnel of light

# The Warehouse

I'm having visions of the cemetery

Gravestones and rusty gates it's getting scary

Names etched in the obituary scribbled in blood

Plasma in a 4-page letter the riddle of love

Daydreamer stare at black skies I see white storms

The tears of God as he cries for earth…His produced life forms

The universe is the factory where humans are made

Mass-produced on assembly lines we all look the same

Warehoused, stockpiled, assembled productions

Welded metal, alloy toys, robotic constructions

Fabricated dipped in metal coated with flesh

Sit on the shelves for decades social neglect

Collect dust in the storage room of irrelevant stock

Life finally makes a sale, you're sealed in plastic, put in a box

Special delivery a fleet of trucks leave Amazon

Drop you off, ring the doorbell, your new home

You been shipped to the ghetto amazon

# The Night I Met Jesus

*Player 1*

Staggering in a dark alley half-drunk vision blurry

I see an odd vehicle uranium dipped V-20 sitting on 30s

He slammed the brakes shocked and startled I dropped my liquor

Glass splinters I see a shadowy figure I start to quiver

Snatched my necklace said get in the car I followed directions

We sped off...zero to 60 in a fraction of a second

*Jesus*

I have a message I want you to deliver it

Signed and sealed you must gather my nation those who are innocent

I'm hunting Satan galaxy wars he's hiding on earth

It's a race you against time you must finish first

You are stuck...there is no turning back...you have been chosen to ride

Know that you may die and there is a lot more than meets the eye

I know you're thinking if God is real, he must have found another planet to love

Because he left you lonely and all alone on a planet of thugs

I watched you running...trying to get home from these murky slums

You feel lost in this holocaust and that is why you turned to drugs

Swore to yourself you'd never make a baby...so you spill your seeds

You must think you're stuck in some sick game...but it's real and you'll see

Recall the signs I have given do you remember that night

The cold August...the hot December...you surrendered your life

I must leave now but I shall return even worse than before

Until then watch for the signs, the weather, the plagues, and the wars

# Reacquainting With Jesus (3 Months Later)

*Player 1*

I'm going mad the last disciple the 13th apostle

In my mind I'm all I got there is no one to follow

These desperate streets stole my childhood killed my dreams

I was forced into manhood look what they did to me

Crucifixion everything I see reminds me of blood

Keep seeing crosses and 6 point stars…a riddle from above

Lost in the spirit world…maze mansion trapped in the helix

Déjà vu I see the Egyptians in the wings of the Phoenix

Oncoming craft…approaches me…at warp speed with music beating

Here comes Jesus engine screaming and tires screeching

*Jesus*

Get in the car war games you know my approach

You belong to the moment when you ride with the ghost

I returned because you were losing strength about to die in the mission

Want something done right, do it yourself, divine intervention

The guy in the back with the African mink and platinum link

That's Michael the archangel fresh out the clink

*Michael*

Truly sorry for the long delay we were chasing death

Just got back from a shootout on Planet X

Should have seen us…these was nothing between us from here to Venus

Or Serena or Jupiter or Pasadena

We drag the spacecraft for light years, 2 blown engines, and 2 flats

With no glass in the front or back…we still made it back

*Player 2*

Been a long summer of prophetic signs and psychic readings

Palm readers trace lifelines trifling seasons

I was born in generation bulimic the hungry species

Our greed is unquenchable we must eat it

Wasted daily, young and rich, but still Black trash

In a White man's world working for free in Alcatraz

I was crippled by a miscarriage an illegal abortion

Suction devices tried sucking me lifeless I fought the extortion

My daughter looks more like my father I know she's going to leave me

Keep having dreams she's gonna crawl off and pretend she was lost

I see a circle of dark souls men in the night

Aggressive banter thug profiles on the verge of a fight

One of the men stood 7-feet tall with impeccable swagger

Rocked a necklace with a talking lion head in his mouth was a dagger

He shooting dice with some young gods to sacrifice

It's eerie how he hustling souls...Poltergeist

Guns on the ground gambling for crosses, chains, and rubies

In all black he looks like Skeletor up under the hoodie

Primitive etchings and tattoos his flesh is scarred

Long sleeves in the summer's eve to hide his scars

He glared at me and said, "Your invited son take your try."

"Take a turn at the table of fortune let's take a ride!"

# The Night Satan Met Me (60 Minutes Later)

*Satan*

Player 2 you crapped out with a fucking 7

You are now forgotten…the bloody forsaken…the unforgiven

You owe me dawg there is no more credit to be given to you

We need blood for a sacrifice…your best friend will do

Don't try to escape I have your picture all over my walls

You are trapped…this is the rest of your life…I own you young dawg

I'm going to drop you off in the ghetto slums with a mask and a mission

When I return the streets should be empty…souls should be missing

And when Jesus visits ignore his lies…he can't save you from hell

You fool…can't you tell from this long hot summer…you're already in hell

You are now a man I been in love with you since you were an infant

Your complexes and your weak mind…I'm going to drive you senseless

I'll be back by the end of the summer to finish the show

Wait for me…don't try to leave…besides you have nowhere to go

# Reacquainting With Satan (3 Months Later)

*Player 2*

I blame god…why did he put me here and paint me in Black

Tell my people in the poverty district I will never come back

From here…the point of no return…destiny is written

I've reviewed all courses of action this is my best decision

Today I read my horoscope my zodiac doubts

That I will live to see tomorrow…so if I must die…I'll die coked out

Loced out on morphine and ecstasy

I'd hook the world on thorazine if it was left to me

Up ahead 2 sinister silhouettes approach me in vests

I forgot…I loss my soul in a dice game…Satan is here to collect

*Satan*

While I was away I heard that they dropped the towers

Forgot to tell you that would occur…a transference of power

My friend here is an archangel on the streets he is called Malachi

Death threats are unnecessary he's ready to die

*Malachi*

I am an assassin with more guns than America

Murderous, death of a nation, they shall hear of us

I'm noid and I see the ploy so I'm here to destroy

We set fire when we come through hide the girls and boys

I got your back…I'm by your side…we must follow the Master

Take my hand…come with me…swallow disaster

*To be continued…*

St. Des trippin false teachin I swallowed my enemy

Satan transformed and put his spirit into a bottle of Hennessey

The snake is in there somewhere…I can sense through the bubbles

French kiss I sucked the serpent now I know I'm in trouble

A mental smog from joy to pain from a boy to a man

I feel strange…sense somebody's watching me…am I a toy in God's hand

The maze of life I know it by heart I've paced it before

Bleeding to death on the 13th floor betrayed by the Lord

I've entered a zone…a cold haze descends like winter

The 1 room in the family mansion I should never have entered

Stop the world I want to get off it's spinning too rapidly

Barricade the bedroom door afraid of my family

Punch the walls slam doors rip down posters

Psychological warfare my prognosis

These walls have ears don't speak a word…remain silent

Welcome to my darkest hour…you are all invited

We are the results of our father's sins early 70's evils

Wild Irish Rose in our bloodstreams injected with needles

One time for the hungry nights as youngsters we cried

Two times for the food stamps that kept us alive

Let's share a toast for the mid 80's when Reagan was shot up

Let's take a shot for the crackaholics that beat on our mommas

How we made it out of maze mansion we never will tell

But know this we are calm as the liquids in the deserts of hell

I don't know why nobody told you the dark secrets

How baby gods birth in the shadows and rise in the Phoenix

Ain't born winners we born sinners stunting for thrills

Hatch out our eggs hunting for meals and something to kill

The level is real…we live life like we born to kill

Natural disasters…man-made…I hope you can feel

Postcards from the other side I try not to read them

Ignore the faces and glowing eyes pretend I don't see them

Murder mystics in magic city the dark dimension

Hocus-pocus holographic thugs narcotic visions

Abracadabra…incantations…a conjuring curse

Like numinous rains the tears of God have flooded the earth

Angels fall and life dies for no reason

Got time to kill and money to burn as if we don't need it

Run on water walk through flames we so higher

Was born too early ahead of time beautiful liars

I want to paint the white sky black like Jesus

Flip flop the whole game the puzzle and pieces

Paper chase this American Dream the tale is fairy

Poetic justice we chant scriptures in solitary

When God pauses to catch his breath…the earth stops spinning

Cars crash, sinners repent, and jump off of buildings

There are 4 seasons and 4 reasons we ride or die

The 7 sins with the 4 devils don't suicide

From drug wars to holy wars to the Omni Code

Sat next to God sorted through files this is the life I chose

It is a game…it is not a real…it is all in the brain

Touch my pain molten hot steel…put it all in your brain

I got foes and I shot those with glock blows

I rock shows I rock roll I got soul

I'm brave still I'm kind of scared so I lock and load

The game is broken…it is wide open…it is not sowed

# Ghetto Hero

Blood in blood out we are not safe

The ghetto hero soars in with his black cape

Plasma rains on the killing fields and quickly ices

Meth crystals teenage gods the black virus

Give the game a slow kiss in the magical forest

Carousels and fairy dust we are trapped in the chorus

Disembodied lost souls with no names

Feel no pain like we been tweaking on cocaine

White rain freezes over the hood…creates black glaciers

Shakespearian lyrics, our life is a movie, our lives are on paper

Understand this is not our home we came from the wires

Holy Ghost initiation we were baptized in fire

Pace in the dark bleeding to death we are half-dead

Until kingdom comes and destiny strikes you shall know dread

This has been the summer of death and prophetic illusions

Psychological warfare we are obsessed with the music

In our world the dead don't die they stalk of the living

High off liquor and holy water trying to find the city

The sons of Satan clash swords with the sons of God

Lightning flashes to the ends of the earth…to the sun and the stars

# Can You Stand The Rain

This is too much joy this is too much pain

This black city took us down we have lost our way

Came as you were I took you that way please never change

I really need to ask you if you can stand the rain

I see you in these ghetto streets trying to push through

You look at me as if you want me to look at you

Are you that fantasy girl from my fantasy realm

Will you please be my girlfriend until the world ends

Do you want to hold hands while we slow dance

Do you want to romance with a grown man

Will you follow love's star and go to war for me

Take my pain away...be my codeine...my morphine

Drunk in love you're in my bloodstream I am your love feign

Love withdrawals bring heart spasms and emotional screams

On desperate nights when we hug you give me a buzz

This is more than physical love...this is chemical love

## The Life And Times Of A Broken Heart

This lady called Love is killing me softly

My whole heart is underwater drowning so awfully

My momma says that I am crazy for enduring your pain

My poppa says I am less than a man for enduring your shame

In the beginning it was so pure...me chasing my angel

It was my passion to reach you first...so I was racing the devil

So emotional I couldn't stop crying so I panicked

Death pact we...said we would die together on love's Titanic

You told me I would never feel like I wanted to die anymore

Told me I would never-ever have to cry anymore

Romantic lies...lullabies in paradise

Told me you loved me as you stared deep into my desperate eyes

You were a little ghetto girl who needed a little ghetto boy

You were all I had...I was all of your joy

But you brought me pain you gave me fire

You held me down I could go no higher

If I had wings I would have snatched you out of the night

Flown you to the moon far-far away to a place beyond this life

We still haven't found what we are looking for it seems

Goodness gracious amazing graces stuck in a reoccurring dream

Life won't stop, the whole world is passing us by

Driving through Memphis running on empty still alive

She walks into my dreams…I talk in my sleep

Euphoria's rapture I am hopelessly lost between the sheets

Call me insane a daydream believer imprisoned apostle

Fairytales and nightmares in my twisted novel

Satan sings to beautiful music in symphonic tragedy

A bad moon is rising amongst dreamy stars shining in our galaxy

Someone blocked eternity's path to the gates of heaven

Highway hypnosis…unrighteous fixations…we missed our exit

We missed our signs wandering hitchhikers on the magic mile

This too shall pass it will all come suddenly crashing down

Life goes on or so it seems like ripples in streams

Echoes from last night's dream silent memories

## Heaven Is On Fire

Our heaven is on fire I know the Lord see it

It is not a bittersweet memory…it is not a long lost secret

It travels in the wind telepathic thoughts travel

Paradise is smothered in flames as desire unravels

We fell in and out of love with God's magical city

We are all shooting stars who crashed through the windows of life's glass ceiling

If I ever was to lose my mind I would still remember this place

I want to go home and make everyday forever…conquer time and space

# Toy Soldiers

Smoke, fire, and flames dust-to-dust...ashes-to-ashes

Seems as if this city is an abandoned village full of lonely bastards

The heart of the city beats heavy like subwoofers

The enigmatic power source of an evil system...it seems life took us

Used and abused in ghettos we have been caged

Slaves to the game chains on our brains

We got no dreams we got no visions

We got one purpose we got one mission

Toy soldier rebels march to the city

March through the city and empty out the city

Leave no names, souls, or faces

Rage against the machine paralyze the matrix

Take no prisoners let none surrender...this is street justice

Without saying nothing we prayed for their destruction

We sung with the angels and danced with the devil

Made black rose petals out of stone cold metal

As infinity's clock stops ticking the earth stops spinning

You shall not receive a graceful ending this is just the beginning

Meteor showers will pour on City Hall...they will be caught in the rain

The whole city will be evacuated...smothered in flames

The wheel in the sky will keep on turning

Since my people are still dying...the city will continue burning

## Dark Project

Kids go to heaven as men go to hell

As there are killers on parole...there are killers out on bail

Ghetto tricksters sleep all winter awake and hustle all summer

Guns flash like lightning and crash like thunder

With a robotic nature...full metal thugs wear full metal jackets

Shooting full metal slugs and filling up full metal caskets

We are all tracked by the system with a barcode matrix

We all have been given numbers that feel like our faces

When the Lord God cries the Satan devil laughs

The mathematics of a bizarre life the numbers don't add

Today the NASDAQ is up but the Dow Jones is down

The stock market is mystically crashing...Wall Street has drowned

Rioters loot set flames ablaze to downtown

A purge...the night of the living dead...it is crazy downtown

Man vs. machine we are coming for the system

Rampagers are burning down temples tearing down buildings

We are more than test-tube babies...although they think we are objects

They put us in the projects but now we are escaping this dark project

# Ghetto Theme

There is a man in the mirror...an eye in the sky

There are cameras in the ceiling...don't try to run...don't try to hide

We can fly to the skies deny all inertia

I am alive you are alive let us not get murdered

Prostitutes turn cheap tricks they do all levels

Always a blue light special for the red light special

These sour slums are candy coated with cream-colored chocolate

We have to fly away on the mothership rocket

The ghetto is on display police go window shopping

The torture of a 1000 faces...trapped in prison cells...inside an evil locket

You can look but don't touch...you can glance but don't stare

White niggas and Black crackers...it's quite obvious these streets don't care

Action figures in hot wheel cars...toy store burglars

Rape the streets with the kiss of death...stone cold murderers

Father Time and Mother Nature must be addicted to pain

Blood on our hands we scurry in frenzies to clean-up the stains

False prophets and dark apostles predict your position

Occultic sacrilege stole enough souls to start their own religion

Death comes first birth comes last

What goes around comes around the future is the past

We breathe easy yet we die hard

Lord Jesus we beg of you my God

Pull the plug on these dark powers

We are lost victims of a dark system

These cribs have roaches these rats have rabies

Pimps pimpsmack ladies and human traffic babies

Raised by our stay at home mommas…deserted by our long-gone fathers

Psychobabble and psychodrama this is life's soap opera

My greatest hope was a peace of mind for just 1 year

Saw all 7 of my deepest fears in 7 moons…how did I get here

All my life what they wanted from me is what they took from me

I'm hearing voices and dark whispers tricking and fooling me

Life is a game I'm doing my best to play this position

A holy war on life's chessboard in the name of religion

# Ghetto Laboratory

It's a quiet storm although it never rains in southern California

This gothic nation is paranormal these people here are not normal

There is something in the water ripples in the rain

Look in the mirror stare at your face and look into your brain

Incubating inside test-tubes and petri dishes for observation

Racially-driven experimental laboratories designed our complication

Tragically living on faith deeply breathing off our prayers

Desperately screaming into outer space is anybody there

The surround sound reverberates acoustics from the heavens

Echoes from other planets in glass chamber sections

Long white jackets greet you at the gates of a man-made nation

Projected images of a virtual ghetto computer generated

If you ever escape on the freeway to heaven you will see death's path

The 49 cylinders of hell beneath the city made of glass

Daydreaming make believing in a fairytale

Picking dandelions touching the clouds on a carousel

"Your Honor, I blacked out so right now I can't remember."

Can I reference the book of life so I can spell it out and paint the picture

Mistakenly bailed out...computer error...it was late December

Or Nevuary...all I know...I was barefoot on the streets in the dead of winter

I needed shoes, I needed jewels, I need a clothes

I needed brews, I needed Kools, I needed blow

I stole a Newport small box to shake the angst...fresh out of detox

Shivering like smallpox...inconspicuous...paranoid like 2Pac

Broke with no bread and no dough

Lonely with no queens and no hoes

Hungry with no cheese and no chips

It was just me and I...we was hit

Them Whiteys didn't hear me coming...they didn't even see me running

I was 3-dimensional in the kaleidoscope of life's 3-D colors

I hit a lick...I slit his wrist...then flew away with the Desert Eagle

Hollow tips echoed in eternity now my conscience wants to murder me

A picture is worth a thousand words

A picture is worth a thousand words

## Stomped Out

They were whooping me, I couldn't breathe, I couldn't see

I couldn't flee, I wouldn't bleed, they wouldn't leave

I started shooting, they started moving, I kept shooting, they kept moving

I kept shooting, I wasn't looking, I couldn't see, I kept shooting

They were player haters, paper chasers, devastators, with dark rages

In the mist of the foggy alley one yelled, "Ha ha...see you in the funny pages."

I heard clicks...I heard shots...so I froze to listen deep...then I ran

Through rush-hour in Chinatown...Chris Tucker and Jackie Chan

I slipped and laid down...and played dead

It's rush-hour at the club again

A human stampede I get off the floor and put my body on the ceiling

I was high off the OxyContin so gone off amoxicillin

Take the pain away

Take the pain away

Dying with purple hearts breathing with iron lungs

Brains covered with metal plates thinking as Native sons

Homicide is no stranger…approach the casket and raise the roof

No fear of what lies on the other side…suicidal yet bulletproof

Murder men with silent weapons in quiet wars

Black rain, black ice, the black Sabbath, the black dawn

We stole blood money from bloody Mary…Hail Mary

We warcraft with warlords who warlock vs. Hail Mary

Follow me through crystal balls…fortunetellers stir witches brew

Over the river and through the woods…from Gun Ru to Englewood

Jump off the roof…crash through the roof…land in the coupe

I play dead slumped at the wheel this is all truth

# Hide From God

You can dance if you want to dance slide on the dance floor

The chants put you in a trance…why won't you dance more

The roof is on fire let it burn in the black night

Can't hide from the Lord in the smoke and the black light

Stuck in a high with the gods of the dark earth

The star and the Lord of lords saved by the lost verse

Race wars beat chasers ride for the Abba side

A day away from the gates of heaven why would you suicide

The house hops when the beat jumps don't stop get it get it

Mesmerized hypnotized don't stop get it get it

6 million ways you can die killer choose one

Life is a movie déjà vu rerun

Suffocating shooting stars run through the escape doors

Stuck in these four walls blood on the dance floor

# Disco Inferno

Pacing in a maze of dark riddles…time tick-tocks eternal

Hypnotized minds burn slow…hip-hop inferno

The speaker box screams through the wires its telepathy

Tragedy meets treachery…agony meets ecstasy

Bass heads bob back-and-forth addicted to the melody

Baked cocaine smolders like anthrax fumes in the balcony

The queen of the night dirty dancing with the sons of man

The prince of the ghetto makes love to a virgin's pants

Pandora's Box unlocked hell's lullaby

Burn baby-burn baby…rockabye rockabye

# Club NuVo

In the darkest of skies there is a full moon…werewolves scream

Welcome to the nightlife terror dome scene

Switch fates with the souls on the dance floor godfather

Baptize souls in the Holy Ghost hot water

I must escape from this reality…I need pain pills…slip me a Mickey

Someone hide me from my vengeful Lord in the tunnels of the big city

Fumbling for the door why is no one trying to help me

Then I realize this place is a hotel…you check in but you never leave

If you listen to the music play you can hear the rhythm dance

Meditate on the squeals and the screeches in eternity's ambulance

Childhood traumas never leave…black minds bleed dark rivers

I see the end of my life and the world in the eyes of the palm reader

Lost and losing in Club NuVo stuck here forevermore

Fallen angels dance beneath the stars…slowing sinking to the Earth's core

Phantom Of The Opera

The stamp on your hand is the mark of the triple beast

The bag in your pants is the poison of the Zulu leaf

There is something over here…over there…oh yes it's everywhere

We'll all live forever just as long as we're all alive in here

Nobody seems to know the name of the song on the stereo

The children of the night pray to God for a miracle

Six dimensional holograms, pentagons, and pentagrams

Pendulums in the purple light swing slow makes us trance

Lured into the belly of the beast manipulated into Babylon

Wrong place, wrong time, in the wrong state of mind

We must escape from this wasteland morph through the Stargate

Crucifixion then resurrection…on day 3 we incarnate

The Phantom of the Opera plays tricks with our destiny

On our 9th life dancing switching fates with the melody

## Andre Rubin's Odyssey To Earth

I was there in Genesis holding the keys in the ovaries of Eve

A seed waiting patient until Revelation to come through her genes

Traveled through the womb of the galaxies…racing Adam's semen

Deranged in the cradle…strangled with the naval…Kane vs. Abel's legion

Racing to reality I killed my twin in self-defense…choked him with the rubber

Half way there still must out run or murder some 10 million others

I truly loved my lil brothers but I felt there were no other visions

That would hold earth down and keep life spinning

Kept my fingers itching engaged to a trigger…not afraid of these niggas

Exchanged fire with crazed killas in a maze of mirrors

I realized…life is a game, life is a test, it keeps testing me

Hanging by a moment…from beginning to end…from luck to destiny

Still racing to reality…through the fallopian galaxy

It sounds so simple but the journey was challenging

I fought with the flames came out choking…I hollered for life

Stressed in mommy's matrix…I came out smoking…poppa gave me a light

Magnetic shields and bright lights I crashed through the stratosphere

Somebody get me out of here…somebody check me out of here

I wander the streets temper boiling on a soulful morning

Moving dope for Constantine…the Black Caesar in the city of Orleans

I'm not hard to find but I am hard to see

Lay in the cuts of the iron mountain…1000 leagues up under the sea

It's so real we're toy soldiers with play doe bills

Sticky wet like sugar water…candy rain on yayo hills

These killers hold steel so don't move an inch you better hold still

Make no frills and no spills when the dealers and the dope deals

Heard a click-click…vroom-vroom…kackow-kackow

They emptying big clips move nigga…move nigga…get down-get down

Tried to fire back…boom-boom-boom…bladow-bladow

Your henchmen are dead…boo-hoo-hoo…what now

Doors slam…we skeeted out…running men in an orange Trans Am

The murder storm is finally over…here comes a rainbow and the ambulance

Coked up on a leather sofa suicidal with a sawed off special edition

Stainless steel semi-automatic I'm about to make the special edition

Special report…the devil is in my kitchen I'm stuck in the television

My biography is a motion picture…a living sentence

My whole life has been a commercial in a movie only God is watching

And only angels applaud…but the devil is the star that keeps stalking

While God is flipping channels…fixing the antenna…checking up on other lives

He forgot about me…He forgot to turn back…He's missing my times

Lights, camera, action…I'm stuck backstage hear my yells

Between 2 worlds parallel hells

It's Helter Skelter in earth's hotel I'm stuck up 6 flights

The man upstairs is playing his music the soundtrack to my life

## Dreamless Sleep

Had a dream I could buy my way to heaven

Woke up and sent 1 million dollars to the reverend

Flushed all my cocaine and ditched the 357

Copped it all back before midnight…before the clock struck 11

Killers need time to kill and hustlers need money to burn

We're blessed by the wheels of steel while cursed by the pills and sherm

Crazy glue is in the reefer

Ears stuck to the ether

My darkest miseries are born out of memories from elementary

Oh my God how'd I live this long…how did I live to see a quarter century

The good die young we rush through life…run-nigga-run

Don't look back now…we came to far…can't turn back now son

Like God I'll die for my children and I will go to prison

To Death Valley on the crucifixes and on day 3 I'll be risen

In paradise with 3 wishes, 3 virgins, and 3 kisses

On my last 3 missions that so futuristic…that is so distant isn't it

I feel young and restless yet forever dying

I had something I wanted to say but nevermind it

Forever fighting and constantly resting in this state of mind

The days are long but the years are short…don't play with time

We all know it is a White man's world but a Black man's culture

And we all know the ghetto is a desert and the cops are vultures

Waiting on the murder scheme

First on the scene last ones to leave

Bet you daddy is going to leave and momma is going to grieve

In these ghettos shooting at the stars the bastards won't bleed

But the earth will die…suddenly explode in the sky

A spinning ticking time bomb…6am good morning Babylon

# Rambling Manifesto

Travel to the 10$^{th}$ Planet within my bedroom walls

I must escape out of this mischievous realm…these walls must fall

I crashed on earth squeezed out of the jam

To save Mother Earth…The Queen of the Damned

She keeps giving birth…it keeps getting worse

Life is a prostitute who keeps getting work

On the 4 corners…lost floors with forgotten doors

Hidden rooms full of dark holes and lost souls

We need more minds we need more rebels

We need more time we need more levels

The book of life, they're skipping chapters, setting traps, and switching actors

I better go home I better go backwards…stuck in the past my future looks blacker

Its deep purple life bleeds fast in slow motion

I believe in the trinity…spirit, body, soul devotion

Put my words in your tears…cry for me…my memory is scorned

Pain is love, God is war, sin is death, a star is born

When the thunder rolls the lightning strikes

We're prepared like Chris Wallace to die tonight

Holy wars and battle cries when will it ever end

I swear to only cry for 2 reasons...death and sin

Mind games, mental wars, and death letters

Daydream fantasy thugs we shall live forever

We thirst to shine like Shangri La metropobecca

Build a ranch on 2 hundred acres and call it mecca

Alibies...I have to lie to get out alive

On level 9 hustling time I'm trying to survive

Made men...made ourselves and raised ourselves

Until this day that's probably why we hate ourselves

We use dope to cope, cocaine for pain, and meth for the stress

Hooked on a feeling, cold hard liquor, and cigarettes

A cold-dog world I stay numb and don't bleed

Pray backwards and lie to God as if He doesn't see

Masonic psalms the school of life will not to fail me

Biowars and atomic bombs will not kill me

We dust and ash in the city of angels addicted to terror

The sands of time I walk barefoot in this American desert

Selling crack to keep gas in the engine of time

Angel wars...flight of the Phoenix...there is a hole in the sky

Quantum leap from ghetto to ghetto mastered the skies

Dream worlds asleep at the wheel traveling time

The last man on this wretched earth I have to be

Machine created reality…it is so divine it is comedy

Dark music from Dante's Inferno…déjà vu

The soul asylum we are all eternal trapped in this cube

Rolling stones and heartbreakers the sins of the fathers

Laugh now and cry later…put seeds in the daughters

Wet dreams I kissed Katrina slow as the ocean

Hallelujah, this is soul food…we live off emotion

## Ghosts Of Mississippi

We leaving on the midnight train to Mississippi

A truckload of crooked eye killers are rolling with me

Drunk driving drinking Davinci and Amaretto

Leather seats reek of cheap cologne and Cigarillos

Slow drag…don't choke on the chronic the car is steamy

Cough syrup is in the glove compartment breathe easy

Hydroplaning calm in the brain we zoom in the rain

Leaned low like Kool and the Gang we screwed in the game

As one team we stare at the state troopers that pass by us

They stare back into our president tints but can't find us

Race wars we ride with the ghost an 8th of a mile

We weighed down…we can't keep up…we are scraping the ground

We tote dope and pots to cook and pot to smoke

The trunk stocked with rocks that look like bars of soap

No pics, no face to match, no license plates to run

No fingerprints, no serial numbers to trace the guns

Poor souls we talk to the spirits in the whiskey

Flying south to bury the ghosts of Mississippi

## Midnight Interrogation

I had a dream tonight is about to last forever

I saw heaven…us in vests bleeding…about to die together

Oh happy day, let us drink away the pain smoke weed to stay sober

There is a message in the bottle and the 4-leaf clover

Our luck is running out the hour glass is empty

Our earth suits are leaking our power packs are dripping

We sing to slow songs…cry like the ocean

Write death letters…talk slow motion

We sing off key harmonize in reversal

Life got us off our square and put us in a circle

Interrogation…surrounded by oil barrels and stacks of magazines

They're screaming, "Who did it?" with matchsticks and a can of gasoline

They ask a million questions we denied all whereabouts

Pistol-whipped us in the mouth cross-examined with the gauge out

They stole our playbook tore every page out

In the crucible of torture we have to find our way out

# Traffic Jam

Black guerrillas tiptoe through the club like some ballerinas

Phantoms of the opera in a creature double feature

You can hear demonic squeals through the wheels of steel

In a haze of fluorescent smoke the clubbers catch the chills

Black lights flicker they like running shadows

We lost our targets in the wind…there they go again

I squeeze in the midst…the lemon trigger blowing

Squeeze the handle like orange juice from Southern California

Bullets rain laced with formaldehyde tips

And cyanide strips and dynamite sticks

There they go again they're crawling on the floors

They are running through the doors now they're running through the walls

My machine guns empty still I chase them in the streets

Full of gas and adrenaline I'm fast and I'm furious

Life is a traffic jam call the ambulance

Now I'm headed back north escaping out of this circumstance

The engine of life is running off fumes

Planet Earth is on fire so I'm off to the moon

# The Revolution Is Here

As all others we just want justice, freedom, equality, and a simple life

Instead, they profile our Blackness, fabricate evidence, and give us triple life

Behold, the latter-day Saints are finally here

The Lord's Day is upon our collective struggle…Saturday is near

The North Star has been summoned, the map is scribed, our plotted escape

The Underground Railroad our allies await…look for our ancestors at the gates

Gather the money and the weapons burn all of the letters to hell

Our God left us a roadmap…a biblical tale…read the verses well

Our advocates have dug holes to freedom we pant slowly inside of funnels

In desperate humility we pray to the heavens inside of hades tunnel

Broke out of our cells underground we dwell…as black masked warriors

A ghetto appeal, no judges, no lawyers, we are force destroyers

## Stained Glass Skies

Legions of angels with halos monitor hoods

A city of devils and pitchforks up to no good

A cold-cold world a dog-eat-dog nation

Soul survivors of Father Time's futuristic arch miraculously postdated

Thug love rapes the hood with kisses of death

Seduced by the street-life enchanted by the allures of sex

No golden crosses just 6-point stars and murder ones

Stain glassed skies block the illuminating rays of the illustrious sun

Sacred clouds hover over cathedrals we worship in the night

Ebony skin and ivory eyes symphonic twilights

A vanilla sky drips chocolate rain…a perfect storm made of tyranny

Cry so slowly…and beautifully…fade to black these are our sweetest memories

My mind's eye has read the password on the Masonic tablet

Look into my eyes and see what I see…hallways to the final passage

Engraved codings on my right palm numinous lifelines

Gypsy ladies and fortune tellers majestically hypothesize

Dead Sea Scrolls plagiarized they hacked our soulful story

Blood, sweat, and tears a beautiful lie stole our miraculous glory

Fly by night crashed momma's car in the field of dreams

Thrown through the window of life's stained glass sky…stuck in a dream

### The Beginning Is Here

At the stoplight in a glass Cutlass with a see-through engine

Invisible man only oxide flames reflect a beatific prism

In the fast lane a swerving ambulance…this world is making me sick

Coughing blood with iron lungs asphyxiated on myths

Hustling time, calorie counting we have lost way too much waiting

Out here starving, we need more meals it has become our fixation

The elitist arms must be stolen by thugs from the Pentagon

Black vigilantes reminiscent of Vietcongs in Vietnam…these streets is ours

From B.C. to A.D. from guerrillas to beings

From lost boys to lords, gangstas, disciples, and kings

Houdini sinks in the sands to find Nephertini

Frantically speeding through hater city in a stolen Lamborghini

Slipped out of consciousness…no concept…exist in the past

Comatosed in the Holy Ghost wishing for a pass

Semiautomatics spilled 3 shells with 1 hammer

Mere men killed God with 3 nails and 1 hammer

2 long scopes and 2 red beams still can't see me

Varsity coach told me I was too street and he just couldn't keep me

In 1 day I lived a life of crime and passion…I ain't lying

So sick of living but like Magic…I ain't dying

## The Puppet Master

To my beloved children, I'd rather let you die then to watch you struggle

This is life and you living it…I guess I got you into trouble

Sweating and shivering in interrogation inside the 5th quarry

It was the devil, he made us do it, stick to the story

In our brains are miniature thugs pulling levers and flipping switches

Control our bodies make us do evil things too sick to ever…mention

Take it to the grave cremated confessions…crashing spirits

These true lies in the black box…my last words are tragic lyrics

Divine appointments I'll meet you there at the end of the story

Parallel cells in heaven or hell no purgatory

In the deepest of slums eating crumbs I keep on the run

Hear mama screaming through the bedroom walls speaking in tongues

Freaks of nature and we might be ugly but we still got feelings

Black sheep, we bleed red, we are still God's children

We go to trial in 30 days we are all on bail

Blood is thicker than the deepest of waters my brothers don't tell

7 wandering spirits multiplied by 7 drifting souls equals 49 cells

Street religion will avenge our karma…pay them back with hell

In the dawn of the full moon we ball in the thunder and rain

Loaded guns and loaded dice the gods of the game

Mercury is rising rapidly dial 911

Been running from the devil like al-Qaida since 911

In the halls of maze mansion praying for my sisters

On the eve of dooms day quoting sacred scriptures

Our neighborhood was injected with heavy metals see the bones in our face

We have lost weight double-crossed by an oppressive fate

God stares at his Black coals we burn fury into his iris

Slaves to the game but masters of time evolving into diamonds

## Florence Nightingale

You bring all my pain I addictively touch your fire

The weight of your love holds me down yet it takes me higher

Fly by night to a place beyond this life

Euphoria's moon whispers...glistens in the night

We came too far to turn back now, I can't give up, I do not know how

Passionately in love with your struggle I wanna be down

You all I ever wanted, dreamed of, or ever needed

The sweetest misery...mystical memories...our darkest secrets

I can't and won't stop loving you

No matter what you say...no matter what you do

I know you don't mean it...you know I never mean it

Our heaven is on fire I know the Lord see it

This love is so good yet it hurts so bad

This love is unordinary but still the best I ever had

I know I never say it because maybe I'm afraid

Just one question on my brain can you end love's pain

It's sickening on all I love I can't think of who

Thickness tensions in the air I put that on you

It's in the wind telepathy your thoughts travel freely

Stars fall through the windows of life's glass ceiling

If I lost my mind…I would still think of you

Lady you know I'm crazy about you…I want babies by you

I want to leave but I do the math…it just doesn't calculus

Brains, body, booty, and beauty…it just doesn't algebra

Love spell kiss your Mack with soft butterfly kisses

So in love, if life is a bitch, I'm stuck in this mistress

I gave you all that I had…the toilet and sink

Now you snatching my chain and smacking my cheeks

You fled barefoot mad in the streets and flagged the police

Arrested, an incarcerated monk now I'm back in the clink

Letters you send begging again to give you a chance

To make pretend it never happened…and just let you back in

Twisted passions bring tumultuous pain and this pain brings pleasure

Heaven is on the way…can we for once talk about something better

Years wasted so many tears you were cruel and unusual

Trigger my switches pushing my buttons making me lose control

The breakdowns, suicide notes, death threats, mental hospitals

If I snap I'm not responsible because anything was possible

It is finished I can't go on…you are too far gone

I can't help you let go of my hand…I want to go home

## Electropsychosis

High off the music stagger onto the stage

Shoot into the crowd bullets ricochet and create a maze

As the lead singer screams the party people sing mass choir

This is their home planet rock…earth, wind, and fire

Microphone fiends they share infected needles chasing a high

Bass heads for dope beats addictive lace is in the rhyme

Slaves to the music melodically chained to the rock and rhythm

The bars and hooks imprison the spectators locked in the system

Hip-hop, trip-hop, acid rock…dance until comatosed

Biologically hijacked chemical war overdosed

Dance gracefully in muddy waters…swamp music tantrum

Hands clap adrenaline rush the wallflower anthem

Change gon' come though it has been a long time coming

We are a long way from Africa let's dance…we've spent enough time running

Call on your maker before the dark shocks you and the shadows craze you

Spit the blood up don't give up the doctors will save you

Def com 3…dropping atomic bombs over Babylon

Fairy tales, magical rainbows, street Leprechauns

The life and times of a gifted orphan…whose God is also his Father

Genesis to Revelation the divine Author

Our Creator who art in heaven let us make a blessed pact

1 thousand years until kingdom comes no less than that

Mark of the beast 3 sixes Stargate dimensions

Curse demons with the 3 sevens arcadia visions

Black males cast dark spells on the culture…black magic

Crawl through the slums then disappear as if white maggots

Symphonies in the synagogue crimes of disastrous passion

Prodigal sons defy the laws of nature...mind-over-matter

The diary of a mad man ink stains from destiny's teacher

Inertia at subatomic levels invisible ether

Infiniti is stuck in a vice versa there is no running back

Machiavellian we've been twice murdered there is no coming back

Slouched in the courtroom stressing and drunken I lied by myself

Came in this world naked with nothing I will die by myself

The universe is the factory where God makes humans

I have no papa thus and therefore I call my father music

The confusion is so organized the water clock pours

It's zero hour the calm before the storm

They wore my mask they're trying to frame me...appeal the verdict

The whole time I was chilling on Venus...I am still a virgin

# Ghetto Trial

My crew was posed on the street corner on the city strip

Loudly declaring to our rival crews, "Y'all ain't shit."

Is all we said as we laughed at them maggots

They were Black trash breeding off our shit

Is all we said as we reminded them that this is our land

Y'all the Indians and we the White man

Y'all had better give us our bread…give thanks for what you're given

We could have manifested your destiny…be thankful that you're living

Is all we said then slowly walked back to the truck

While the slow bass grooved and oozed out of the trunk

Then something started moving there was something in the bushes

Something started shooting villains started pushing

Then they appeared we faded to black in broad day

They disappeared we circled to the back…the long way

We reemerged like ghost riders in hell's wind

We re-converged on a one way street it was a dead end

We disengaged, switched vehicles, and came back

Then reengaged with different clothes but the same gats

Reappeared out of nowhere like human nature

They disappeared in thin air as if human vapors

Found innocent self-defense stood our ground

Street religion, street justice, a ghetto trial

## Flower Child

Love spell I'm hooked like a cocaine addict

Majestically addicted to your dark allure and strange magic

Enchantment, romantically slow dance in the waterfalls

Game rushing straight to my head…a passionate Tylenol

We bumper to bumper life is truly a traffic jam

Soul whipped I'm a slave to your master plan

Don't ever tell me anything that you can't prove to me

Whisper to you what I want to hear…Spit my game back to me

Abricka dabricka I'm asking you something so be quite

Holy shazam what would you do for the pink diamond

Be my superfriend, superfreak, chocolate supermom

Supersonic, sonicboom, sista you are the bomb

# Dante's Inferno

A new era, a new tomorrow, a new world order

A new form of revolution…a new hood order

The dark omen the terror aura the holy horror

The underworld Temple of Doom…the murder slaughter

It all started in maternity ward I was born on drugs

Galvanized in mercury floods a storm of slugs

Elementary was like penitentiary I fought for my food

Hunger games…war games…it was not a game

No clues and no rules we stuck in the wom

Time sit still earth don't move déjà vu

They took my picture snatched my spirit gave it to Satan

Now I know he somewhere watching somewhere waiting

To steal, kill, and destroy the vulnerable child

It so ill these innocent boys are fatherless childs

Buried in unmarked graves sons of the sword

Adopted by the universe sons of the Lord

Young, rich, and beautiful bleed black forever

Crush the republic liberty land is a cold desert

Lust for the night New Jerusalem's glass manger

My Jewish niggas get out of the ghetto…it is a gas chamber

# Super Citizen

The super citizen soars in the night drunk off whiskey

Fly 100 proof with the doors open in suicide city

Bless the dead…shoot up the block with a Tek Rugger

Leaned back in the Lex bubble as if Lex Luger

Look in the rearview mirror popped collar he roars with his eyes

Kryptonite…shoot down supervillains …the Lord of the Flies

Soul controller through wavelengths via Motorola

Tel Aviv sniped long-range remote controller

Believers…we think he's everywhere…the eye in the sky

Watching you intensely when you cock your brim…when you ride and you die

Breathing fire he reigns terror on metropolis city

Cape crusader for the citizens…villains have no promise of pity

# A Civil Rebellion

On cold lonely nights I cry for no reason

Money power respect I will die for street reasons

Who's out there? There is somebody somewhere

Something appears in the silent night then disappears

Cocaine chronicles frozen brains feel no pain

Vanilla skies white lightning cold rain

Ready to leave this cold world doesn't deserve me

Was born too early ahead of time...don't fit in this journey

Condemned to the slums alibies and a life a crime

Teachers meant well when they frankly told me...I was a waste of time

Hopeless myths, I feel like crying, I feel like dying

Broken wishes, I feel like homociding, I feel like suiciding

Princess why you believe in these people they just keeps lying

Queen why are you wiping your tears when you can't stop crying

You seem fearful for your melanin sons and mahogany daughters

Abandoned orphans on a spinning planet with no fathers

If I wasn't Black...I'd move to Iraq...to buy guns and sell crack

Finance an army then travel back on camel back

Hijack the lobby of the federal building...bombs strapped under Avirex

Unmarked packages special delivery anthrax

Politicians need a new message to download

We've been pushed to the ledge...over the borderline...at a crossroads

# The Last Shall Be First

Automatic weapons…momma is in depression

Ain't no payback Karma is in recession

Laugh now no yang laugh later

Never say never until you enter bliss happily forever

6 feet deep to the deadness…to the redness…to the whiteness

To the spirit world, to the lifeless, you may see his image, you might see his likeness

Spellbound by the illustrious brightness

The light at the dark end of the tunnel of silence

That can turn a peaceful man violent

Make him strike a deal with the devil sacrifice the righteous

Passion for the Christ…erase the Judaist scriptures

Obsessed with street religion and the stars of the Egyptians

Men vs. gods…unity vs. segregation

The moral of the story is somewhere between Genesis and Revelation

Government treachery…crack cocaine gave us low IQs

Central Intelligence and Federal Bureaus don't play by moral rules

Looked over they thought we were slow…special needs

Shamed…labeled 3rd world…a social disease

Neglected seeds aborted legions the prophets lied

A Black civilization dehumanized but in the end…immortalized

---

## Murder Mystique

Woke up turned 21 I'm finally a man

Separate the haters and pawns foes from friends

On cloud 9 in the ozone chemically flying

Then I realize I celebrate a horrid day...I'm closer to dying

At subzero waters too cold bloods too thick

Life is a thug stuck with the gun running too quick

Throw stones in a glass house in the concrete jungle

Forcefields evading death in a Teflon bubble

40 days and 40 nights time moves slow

Prepare to enter the Twilight Zone welcome home

Bloody Madonna, Dark Medusa, change the truth

Teleport from the Vatican to Mount Zion's roof

Wandering soul dream-to-dream...through Aquadas

The Asiatic puppet master, the Rasta Fah

My platinum cross swings parallel centrifugal motion

Hypnotic piece stare deep into the froze ocean

Lean forward hypnotized by sacred jewels

An avatar I change colors as the sun moves

Shot 5 times still I rise street respected

Recharge during solar eclipses electric genetics

Fell in love with a ghetto princess our palace is the street

She loves me for who I am...a child of the beast

# Let The Dead Bury The Dead

Demons 3 sixes...angels 3 sevens

In the dark dazed and confused help us find heaven

Reality is fantasia...blink your eyes...take another look

Not what it seems secret chapters in hidden books

We can't sleep so we don't dream visionless futures

JFK in his motorcade with Martin Luther

I prophecy we shall multiply hustle and violence

Brains powered by strange powers rocket science

Revenge of the nerds terrorize the higher powers

Brick road to the underworld the final hours

God's blood burns with eternal fury

Create the future...organized confusion...Big Bang Theory

Hieroglyphics and Morse Code ancient mummy scrolls

Doom later as if tomb raiders cursed souls

## Phobic Apostle

Sentenced to life I shall return before the end of the season

Court of appeals rush the prosecutor kicking and screaming

Legend has it that thugs die cry when wounded

Call on mommy and Jesus' name as they enter the trauma unit

Hood doctrine...ghetto prophets roll the dice

Paranormal...unnormal...poltergeist

God smears life's coloring book with Crayola creations

Drowning souls...oceans of fire...eternal cremation

Ghost riders haunt the projects warlord men

Insane kids playing to win this game of sin

Black magic, chocolate voodoo, dark charms

Soulish terror on the Ouija board be alarmed

Half-human half-machine a crossbreed wedding

The end of days...Omni Code...Armageddon

Spiritual warfare with social ammunition

Intuition and forewarnings...premonitions

# Passwords And Prophecies

Stare into the light put your ear to the speaker

I shall lead you to the light…the prophet and the preacher

This White man's world making me colder and colder

Hardened by hard times a chip on both shoulders

A grenade is in my hand an AK in my lap

God bless the child who holds his own traveling on this map

America…be aware we are many…we are millions

War games…apocalypse…infinity…Maximillian

Fight to the death no retreat no surrender

They will become believers they will feel us they will remember

The choice, the battle, the saga, the fight

The voices, the whispers, the shadows, the night

Ghost faces lost souls spirits disembodied

The chambers…the dungeons…the grim reaper…the Gotti

Better pray to God that He see you and He blesses you

That He lets you out the game before He tries you before He test you

Sadistic street religion where the psalms bleed

Decimate our enemies in the coming century

Illuminati holds the secret the code of the Messianic

The pyramid…the eye…the eagle…the dollar

It is coming it is law…it is written

The man in the mirror oh my God it was predicted

Hood revered…the #1 stunner…the 9th boy wonder

Bring the lightning and thunder…Christ's lil brother

The spring before the summer running in a Hummer

The Joker blowing laughing gas out the dual mufflers

Intoxicate the streets with oxide nitrous fumes

Left unconscious in the family estate the quiet room

Rabies shivering and sweating silver bullets

Obsessive vengeance the minimum is execution

In slum village slave town chocolate city

It's pulp fiction a nursery rhyme as if kamanichi

Incarnated on our 9th life on a karma license

Calculated…dissect the game with ghetto science

Hollywood…lights, camera, action I finally get the picture

God put me here on a lost cause…on a suicide mission

For light years, I traveled time planet-to-planet

At the speed of light resist the laws of reality's standards

Muddy waters in the dirty south the sands of time

Another world…all my children…the days of our lives

No soap operas, no comic books, no false sagas

No fairy tales, no storybooks, no false dramas

No science fiction, no fake religion, no counterfeiting

No funny money, no false flagging, no happy endings

# Natural Born Killers

Mullah movers, mob ties, Mafioso

Street gangs stand in the rain slanging Cali Cocoa

Now we are really deep in ghetto waters

We see the sergeant more frequent than we see our fathers

Tell me that is not heartless…that's so Godless

Ghetto orphans perpetually homeless

Struggling…living on prayers and pipe dreams

Trying to survive until 16 supplying dope feigns

Stirring crack in the Bat Cave in the dark basement

All in the game and we all hate it…faded and jaded

The Judaist mob…we were all betrayed there was nothing sacred

Blood stains, graffiti, and tears the block is tainted

Who will save us from these vials of wrath and these 7 seals

God, I know you gave it your all…but did you seal the deal

Used your 1st born for a human shield

Now we spinning wheels…now we seeking thrills

Now we homicidal…now we burning Bibles

Now we under pressure…now we chase survival

Ghetto evolution…ghetto retribution

We are out of answers…we have no solutions

Now we hunt for meals…now we rob and steal

Yes we love Jesus…but we were born to kill

# Cockroach Resilience

Life looks like its throwing sticks and stones

The world looks like a rolling stone

Abandoned houses look like Stone Henge homes

This urban plight speaks all languages Rosetta Stone

But somehow we found gold in this lost city

We found beauty…but it wasn't pretty

The whole world they didn't want us

But we kept coming like cockroaches

We got scars and tattoo tears

We got broken hearts for souvenirs

Not a turf war…not a gang war

Not a drug war…it's much more

They are trying to take us out…while we're still living

40 days 40 nights striking distance

Just take me away from these White racists to the Serengeti

In a midnight black Mercedes

Fantasize about a world much better

Wet dreams in the middle of the desert

Shooting dice with the demons and the angels

Hustling souls like Casino Royale

Live for the moment and right now I just want to be free

In the box doing triple life with 1 CD

On repeat until my soul feels me

They don't know who we be…they don't know who we be

## Beastly Marks

Sitting in a black room full of Black dudes

With teardrop tattoos gorillas with attitudes

In a maze full of stacked cubes shaped like the Pentagon

Megatrons and Decepticons in the Land of Oz

Barcodes and microchips embedded in the back of our wrists

Tracking devices…database…mainframe…we are on the guest list

We are on a death wish Helter Skelter in the city of God

Long kiss goodnight…die slow breathe hard

Dark gods, hot rods, cop cars, dark dawns

Glock scars, hearts charred, rock stars

No love…throw slugs

Walk dead…on drugs

A rebel with 1 cause live for another breath

Survival at all cost the price for life is death

Running on rooftops leaping for heavens steps

We shine bright, the blackest diamonds, shimmer like crystal meth

Give me life or liberty we stuck in these ghetto streets

Fist fight with the shadows of death…no justice…no peace

This world's heat is so fiery it is making my soul ice

Ex-cons and choirboys we are going to paradise

They're trying to give me with the maximum sentence on flaws

They're trying to lynch me because I'm Black, I'm rich, and I'm Don

Send in the copters in the black of the mist of the fog

Shot down my chopper now I'm climbing the fence in the yard

Ducking and hiding…they're sending in troopers and dogs

Running on empty I won't fall I'm true to the cause

Rubber gloves, no clues, fingerprints, or probable cause

Won't stop for breath until I'm back in the hood with my dawgs

Hide in the forest with the wood, and the leaves, and the logs

Pray to the heavens, the moon, the Ru, and the gods

Been on fire, since the womb, to the tomb, to the mosque

I can't lose, I refuse to move, I won't be a pawn

## From Beyond The Grave

Countdown speak these last words in this hour to live

Donate my heart to the Blue Shield…give mines to a kid

Don't worry about me save yourself I'm shot in the mission

We'll meet again on the other side…the outer dimension

I'll rain ice and dollar bills to my infamous team

Fist fight with the hands of time in infinity's ring

Contaminate the world's water with bioterror

Blow rose petals, rain cold metal, from the sky pull levers

Greet my nation with white doves and a holy kiss

Show me love with leather gloves…clinched black fists

Should have been careful what they wished for on those silent nights

Because Michael and his 7 angels are about to ride tonight

# The Lost Boys

You are listening to dead men talking

You are traveling with dead men walking

In this slow rain drizzling cocaine

It's so cold snowy veins

Cross breed with the demon race

There is a whole in our hearts an empty space

We been burglarized and murderlized

Aborted legions…spermicide

Visionaries what we see is scary

Broken memories…frozen cemeteries

Dying so slow living so fast

Traveling so slow moving so fast

With no doors and no glass

On the highway of life with no gas

At a crossroad with no path

With no words and no math

Take a look at our dark souls see through we

Lost boys running in a horror movie

## Life's Casino

Concrete cold cells

Steel chains it's so real

It's so ill it's so sick

It's so skinny it's so thick

Never high always sober

In these hallways this dark coma

I can't breathe I can't eat

I can't dream I can't sleep

Pull the plug cut the wire

Set my soul on fire

Nevermind we're in Neverland

I ain't never lied…I ain't never said

I was immortal a bulletproof superman

The pistol is in my lap…the pistol is in my hand

The pistols to my head, so emotional

Rollerscoasteral, so unsociable, so unapproachable

Flirting with death excitation

Buried alive suffocation

Gambling souls…a pair of dice

7-11…paradise

Bet it all hustling dreams

1 more silver dollar for the slot machine

In life's casino pull the lever

Pull the trigger…never say never

## Family Mansion

A cold lonely cell with fiery bars

Barbwire fences surround the yard

My family mansion is a ghost town

Love don't live here it don't come around

Afraid to make a sound only soft whispers

My silent screams swim in hard liquor

In this home there are rooms with holes in the walls

On every single floor there are doors leading to scars

Behind every door there are stairs leading nowhere

On the 13th floor sits a man in a chair

Slouched over with his head in his hands

Lost in his brain…pacing the maze in his head

Praying to the dead to the spirits for a spell

Don't tell heaven or hell…about my family mansion's tales

# Prodigal Sons

Speed racing on the run in tequila dawns

Daredevil chasing Medusa's demon spawn

Been on the run in this storm my whole life

Disadvantaged with a knife in a gunfight

Gunplay pray to God that it's Sunday

We will fly to the sun children one day

Game pieces on the chessboard chutes and ladders

Candyland fairytales ain't no miracle answers

No gleeful ends so we make pretend

Cursed seeds suffer hard because of our daddy's sins

From slave town, to plantation city, to peasant village

Disturbed fury in need of emotional healing

Pedal to the metal turbo through the city streets

Americans vs. Afghans the depths of beef

Burn rubber evade cops tires squeal

Patrol cars flip, loose grip, can't hold the wheel

Off road use a corpse for a human shield

Silent rain quiet storm in the killing fields

The Clash of the Titans detonated bombs

1 man army fragments of God

# War Thirsty

True life the reality of human nature

Galaxy wars in the solar system Stargaters

White vultures circle the ghetto hover our town

The same hood over and over merry-go-round

The omen…Satan's playground…subculture

Underworlds…valleys of hades…cold torture

Mayhem rushing through life feigning heaven

Quadruple life, murder ones, 187

Wonder why the hood is hungry, dark, and thirsty

God's still mad they killed Jesus…Lord have mercy

These war stories are epic sagas of senseless drama

We owe karma ominous aura life's soap opera

Obsessive…overwhelmed don't get too close

Compulsive…adrenaline rush on impulse

Repay our masters with dark prayers and dooms day scriptures

Blow Molotov kisses and love letters…birthday wishes

Treacherous venomous doctrine…they shall escape to Mars

This is the war to end all wars…these streets are ours

# Cowboys and Indians

Cocaine cowboys smoking Indian pyro

Italian Lambo with a Pilipino breezo

Diversified Negroe…multicultural lingo

Get in where you fit-in learn to mingle

Looking through peepholes we are not blindfold

Dog-eat-dog world made us trifle and ice cold

Look into our black soul you will see a black hole

A black door with a portal that leads to a trap floor

Steel chains cause membrane shift

Turn insane, maniac, flip the script

You can lose 9 lives in this arcade

Lose your last man playing life's game

Don't ask me…blame your God

This is not a game don't play your cards

They got loaded decks and loaded teks

Death threats, crystal meth, generation X

X-cons X-men X-addicts

Sex, drugs, and hip-hop…street ballets

Hallelujah vex the world with a White man's hatred

Steal land and kill spirits…call it sacred

We chase dreams like White teens on Elm Street

Fred Kruger we travel in sewers beneath the streets

America's nightmare don't sleep through it

Running in a scary movie this is the theme music

Born on the 4th of July torn from my momma at 5

I fell through the hole in the sky

Magical powers summon God's mystics

Separating truth…the fact from the fiction

Superstitious running through a mirrored portal

Our life spans are cut short but spirits soar immortal

It's Black Friday, Halloween, and demon night

Satan standing up ahead in my headlights

If you could feel how I feel you would probably cry

If you could kill God's will you would suicide

Galaxy wars, storm troopers, starship enterprise

Escape from earth and this Black god genocide

Survival of the fittest long live the strong

Earth, wind, and fire…universal laws

# The White House Scandal

Under pressure house full of alcoholics

Cigarette butts floating in a broken toilet

Ain't no sunshine in metropolis

Rainbows are colorless in Annapolis

Hopeless souls won't parole from metal bars

Ain't no yellow brick roads to this ghetto Oz

Cartel, gangland, dead presidents

POTUS on payroll...mob ties...federalist

Democratic...bleeding hearts...socialists

Republican...Reaganomics...capitalists

80's babies the crack era stole our homes

Project babies in detox having withdrawals

It's time to riot, loot the city, and torch buildings

Kidnap public officials...street politicking

## Not Guilty

Unpredictable unexplainable unimaginable

Impossible unthinkable unfathomable

Not guilty all defendants found innocent

Plead our case now we're free from this predicament

No visits, no tears, no letters, no sentences

No appeal, no re-dos, no penitence

# Nuclear Rebellion

Coming back to our nation's dark sequel

Freedom train underground until we are all equal

Renegade…rebel slaves…no longer captured

Return of the Mack…teleportation…divine rapture

**Civil rights, Black Power, Black gods**

**This is for Rice, Bland, Garner, and Trayvon**

Malcom X by any means necessary

Dead or alive…riot gear…we will no longer tarry

**Make no mistakes do not misremember**

**We are not prisoners we will not surrender**

In this holy war…this cultural holocaust

Changing the world with atomic bombs…nuclear assaults

# Blame Game

Dear momma where's poppa

Tough luck and misfortune where's karma

Where's God I see Satan

I see the odds I see faces

I hear voices I sense shadows

Do not disturb I'm in battle

Catch a case catch a charge

Get life on Mars behind bars

It's not fair, they don't care, it's a shame

We never had chance I blame the game

I blame God and Satan's children

I blame racism, colonialism, and the state prison

## A Cursed Summer

100 miles and running barefoot in the dessert

Pursue the Grim Reaper chasing an obsession

Jesus take the wheel before I crash the mission

Received a life sentence fled the courtroom unrepentant

Existing in the past, future, and the present

Staring deep into the solars waiting on a message

Blood, sweat, and tears…we keep a tally

Good, bad, and the ugly…Death Valley

The earth suffers a cursed summer

Sons touch daughters and birth mothers

With no fathers…immaculate conception

There ain't no wonder why these lil brothers act reckless

All hope lost…gone with the wind

Ashes-to-ashes dust-to-dust…the wages of sin

# The Moment Before Death

Lost in the forest in the mystic zone

The sacred lands before time was ever known

Fading unconscious slowly sinking into a coma

Angels start applauding I can sense that it's over

God stops trying my family starts crying

A senseless act of violence my boys start lying

The truth be told I had a weary soul

I was ready to go 6 feet below

Graveyard shift my tombstone reads, "He was a secret."

Jehovah's spy, a soldier of light, in heaven's legion

The cemetery breaths slowly moves in the mist

Evil spirts chase trapped souls…ghosts do exists

Werewolves howl…serenade for the broken child

A silver moon dances with the clouds…it's finally over now

## Follow The Light

New world testament messianic crosses

Mysterious monsters, twisted scriptures, false prophets

Astrological horoscopes this is the moment of truth

Bleeding psalms, apostolic doctrines, show me the proof

So real all nations shall feel doom

If pain is love, kiss your bride, enter the honeymoon

Bachelor party fornication in the savage garden

Forbidden fruits the sons of Eve shall not be pardoned

Daydream believer on my last man…my 9th time living

Wandering soul from the outer worlds…the 6th dimension

Black holes to the fiery gates of hades lair

Eternal fury and infinite tears mortals beware

Not make believe, you shall believe, be not deceived

Before you cease to breathe…you shall see

No fear…it's all in your mind…it's all in your brain

Warring for eons with the dragon serpent…he throws flames

Restless rebel with no cause

Russian roulette playing with death…deal my cards

Altered state this the secret path the other way

Forgotten men follow the light ignore what mother say

# We Are GODZ

God complex, delusions of grandeur, as we alter reality

Made men seeking eternal glory…a gangsta's mentality

Guerilla warfare, navy seals, street platoons

Silent weapons for quiet wars in torture rooms

Lords of all thrones we create history

Bring murder rain with hurricanes viscously

Wild kingdom no room for the weak minded

Hero thugs with super slugs…Leonidas

300…much less of us but we are hard to kill

We came up from nothing…God is real

From a ghetto maze…to the devil's chains

From rebel slaves…to renegades

From the 1st page…until the last days

We'll be forever praised…forever in the game

## Moving Sidewalks

Ignore the voices they are Geminis 2-faced

They yearn our fatal wound self-inflicted in momma's basement

Speaking voiceless, wandering helpless, existing faceless

Closed casket, vanished essence, life-force traceless

Black Madonna birthed a Black Jesus sent Him to God's children

They stripped Him, left Him for dead, in the name of religion

Jealous hearts lust to gun us down with badges and triggers

Chasing from behind screaming, "Die nigger...die you niggers!"

Hustling backwards, they put escalators in the concrete

The land of moving sidewalks and repressive streets

In a storm made of glass our umbrella is hope

Love don't hurt or so they tell us in quotes

A dark window peering through black glass

Staring deep into a black moon that hides a black past

A shooting black star births a black sun

A screaming black daughter births a black son

Only saw our moms…never saw our fathers

Only saw bars…only saw the sergeant

Only saw pigs…only saw coppers

Never saw books…only saw copters

Pretty boy thugs for role models, we ran away from home

Married the game, got a divorce, now engaged to stardom

The prison system is an illegal maze the scales of justice must tip

The courthouse has stolen more souls than a slave ship

The X-con state of mind we must break out of this prison

Tell our moms and baby moms to do not visit

Or write letters…what else can we do we but walk on water

Pray to the father…forgive our fathers

Marry our mommas…escape our abortions

Reverse our fate…reversal of misfortune

The Lord is our Shepard we shall not want less

As we walk through the valley of the shadows of death

We shall fear no evil or dusk

For thou art with us and we are with us

Our cup runneth over with supernatural trust

Don't ask us where we are heading…simply follow us

*The end............for now.*

.negrophobia.

# THE INSTITUTE
# OF
# AFRICAN AMERICAN
# PSYCHOLOGY

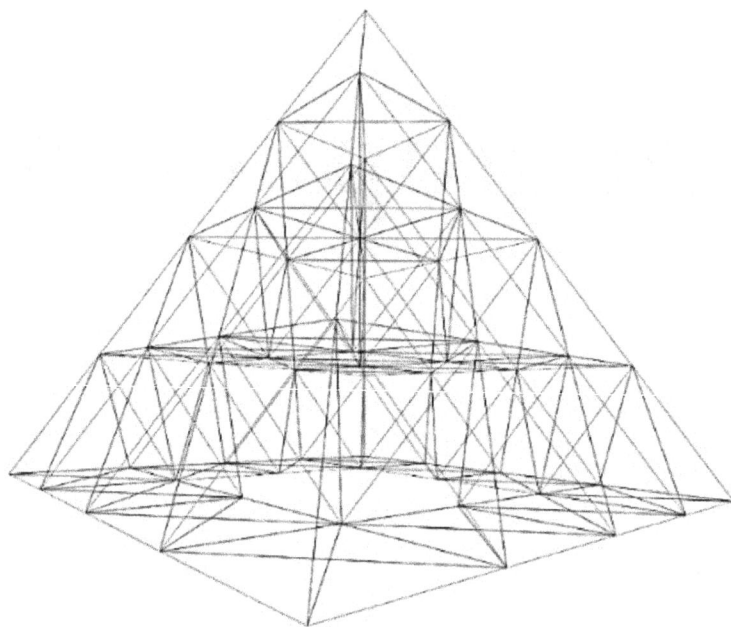

## (IAAP)

www.theiaap.org